PHILOSOPHICAL

AND OTHER TEXTS

DENIS DIDEROT

TRANSLATED BY

KIRK WATSON

DEISI.

Someone who Believes in
God But does not follow any
Religion.

Table of Contents

TRANSLATOR'S INTRODUCTION

Although the young Diderot had been destined for the clergy, he soon lost his faith and, in the spirit of his hero Voltaire, adopted the title of "deist", as well as "skeptic". The *Philosophical Thoughts* has been called "a short manual of skepticism"[1]. In this, his first original work, first published in 1746, Diderot set out to combat the twin enemies of superstition and atheism.

His title seems to confirm this goal, recalling as it does the titles of two well-known books of the age: Pascal's *Thoughts*, first published in 1669 with many later editions, and Voltaire's *Philosophical Letters*, published in 1734; note that this book's title has customarily been translated as *Letters on the English*). Thus, Pascal is set up as the emblematic enemy and Voltaire as the protagonist, the preeminent atheist-slayer (for more information on Voltaire's anti-atheism, please see my translation/collection *In God's Defense: Writings on Atheism*).

First, the enemy: Pascal was a Jansenist. This theological and ecclesiastical movement and the controversy linked to it in from the mid-1600s until well into the 1700s is an essential part of the context for the present book. By adopting Jansenism, a large section of clergy and laity in the Catholic Church had accepted a strict Augustinian reading of Church doctrine which had much in common with Calvinist, i.e. Protestant theology, but was very much out of favor with the Church hierarchy in Rome. In 1653 and again in 1713, the Pope issued Papal Bulls, or official statements condemning Jansenism and its teachings.

---

[1] Morley, *Diderot and the Encylopedists*, Vol. 1, page 44.

Jansenism resisted these moves from Rome, leading to a protest movement which had a penchant for claiming divine mandate as displayed in a string of miraculous cures received by its adherents. Pascal himself had written in his *Thoughts* that miracles are "the foundation of religion" and that "it is not possible to have a reasonable belief against miracles" (*Thoughts* 814, 825), and his own niece had benefited from a miraculous healing. New life was breathed into the movement in 1725 when a woman was healed by taking Communion from a Jansenist priest. Soon after, a certain tomb in a cemetery on the outskirts of Paris became the center of the agitation. Hume wrote in 1748 that "there surely never was a greater number of miracles ascribed to one person, than those, which were lately said to have been wrought in France upon the tomb of Abbé Paris, the famous Jansenist...The curing of the sick, giving hearing to the deaf, and sight to the blind, were every where talked of as the usual effects of that holy sepulchre"[2] In addition, some present at their gatherings would fall into epileptic "convulsions", thus giving rise to their nickname "convulsionnaires". They also became known for the practice of *secours*, "relief" or "release", which involved beating, cutting, and in some cases *crucifying* those who endured the convulsions, all of which was quickly outlawed and prosecuted.

In the *Philosophical Thoughts* these miracles, these extravagant and fanatical practices, which had been going full steam in the decade before Diderot wrote, were still practiced, albeit furtively, at the time of its publication in 1746. In the face of such enthusiasm for the miraculous, Diderot encourages us instead to put faith in cold rationality—he claims that he trusts his judgment more than his eyes—that showing him a miracle will fail where an argument will win him over (section 50). If miracles can be done by a true religion, they can also be done by a false one: an argument that works for both sides really works for none (section 55).

---

[2] *An Enquiry Concerning Human Understanding*, Section X.

So much for the war on superstition. Diderot's other ambition for the book is, in the Voltairean tradition, to weaken the atheist position. Referring to recent scientific discoveries, he was convinced that the terrain for the war on atheism was no longer to be conducted within traditional philosophy but by reference to observational science (section 17). He invests heavily in the argument from design—i.e., the presence of intelligence in the apparent design of the universe, and he regards germ theory and contemporary microscopic science as having undermined the materialist foundations of atheism (sections 18 and 19).

In addition to negating the Christian idea of God, he presents a positive, deist view of God's nature: God is no brutal, punishing monster, nor does He leave us entirely alone (which is still a common misunderstanding of deism) (section 10): "We do not emphasize His presence very much. We have banished God...break down these walls that hold your ideas in, and magnify God: you will see Him in every place where He is": we should see God as our constant companion (section 26).

This book is said to have been rushed onto the page between Good Friday and Easter Sunday in 1746, on the anniversary of Christ's Passion, appropriately enough, since he begins the book by praising the passions: i.e., the strong drives; the counterweight to reason. Diderot makes a strong case for the passions in paragraphs that read like something out of Nietzsche. He praises the passions as a trustworthy guide to the good life, provided they are set in harmony and balanced to produce an optimal outcome—an enlightened hedonism.

This collection also contains a later work, the *Additions to the Philosophical Thoughts*, and a pair of *Unpublished Thoughts,* in which Diderot focuses more and more on Christian teachings, thoroughly debunks the idea of revealed scripture and draws the terrifying real-world consequences latent in some Christian dogma. The *Excluded Thoughts* also contains an interesting fable in which the very idea of God is concocted and spread as a supreme act of revenge on the world by a misanthrope.

Also translated and included here is *On the Sufficiency of Natural Religion*, which pits "natural religion" or deism against all revealed religions, over the course of two dozen arguments arguing that the revealed religions offer nothing that is not already contained in natural religion. This text is rich in information on the deist worldview and contains a fascinating and inspiring conclusion that displays the ultimate political hopes of this Enlightenment thinker, foreshadowing the socialist utopias of the succeeding generations.

It is worth remembering that Diderot suffered for his writing (he was imprisoned for writing a later book): the *Philosophical Thoughts* was condemned by the Parisian *Parlement* (the local face of the *Ancien Régime*) a month after its publication. The book was ordered to be shredded and burned, and the author to "suffer a punishment whose example will terrify [his] peers." A translation of the text of this *Ruling* has also been included in this edition.

PHILOSOPHICAL THOUGHTS

1746

PISCIS HIC NON EST OMNIUM

(This fish is not for everyone)

Quis leget haec?
(Who will read this?)

-Persius, Satires I

I am writing about God. I expect few readers, and I do not think that many will applaud what I write. If these Thoughts *please none, they might be worthless; but I would reject them myself if everybody liked them.*

I.

The passions are always under attack; we blame all our problems on them, while forgetting that they are also the source of each and every one of our pleasures. They are a part of our constitution that we can never fully praise, nor can we ever blame them enough. What annoys me is that nobody ever says anything good about them. Do we think it an offence against reason if we say something good about its rivals? Only passions—great passions—can raise the soul to greater things. Without these, say goodbye to everything sublime, both in morals and deeds; the fine arts become childish and virtue is minimized.

II.

Moderate passions produce only the commonplace. When my country is in danger, and I let the enemy advance, I'm just an ordinary citizen. My friendship is only circumspect, if when he faces danger I'm more concerned about my own situation. Is my own life dearer to me than that of my mistress? Then I'm not much of a lover.

III.

Deadened passions are degrading to extraordinary men. Constraint annihilates the greatness and energy of nature. Think of a tree: we only get that long, cool shadow because it grows wild; you will enjoy its shade until winter comes to clip its locks. When superstition prematurely mortifies the emotions, then bid farewell to all excellence in poetry, painting, and music.

IV.

Then, you might ask, aren't strong passions a good thing? Yes, of course, as long they pull together. Set up a harmony between them, and allow no disorder. When hope has been balanced by fear, affairs of honor by a lust for life, and pleasure-seeking by a regard for health, we will have neither libertines, nor daredevils, nor cowards either.

V.

What utter madness to suggest that we can rid ourselves of the passions. What, should someone wear themselves out, striving to arrive at a state in which they desire nothing, love nothing, and feel nothing? They would become a monster.

VI.

Can I praise something in one man which I begrudge in another? No, of course not: truth, not whim, should be my standard. I must not take what one man does to be wrong, when I think the same thing is virtuous when someone else does it. Shall some people only be allowed to practice certain deeds of perfection, which nature and religion ought to inspire equally in everyone? By no means: where do they get the right? If Saint Pakhom was right to withdraw from humankind and live alone, it must be right for me to do likewise: by imitation I shall gain all his virtues, and I can't imagine why countless others should not have the same privilege. But what if an entire province, sick of the pitfalls of society, and seeking to sanctify their lives, ran off to live like wild animals in the forests: what if a thousand meditation-pillars were erected on the ruins of the sociable affects: a new generation of Stylite monks, religiously stripping all natural affection away, ceasing to be men and becoming statues, to finally become true Christians.

VII.

What a noise! What cries! What groans! Who locked all these wailing cadavers in these dungeons? What crimes did these wretches commit? Some beat their chests with stones, others tear themselves with iron claws: all of them have regret, pain and death in their eyes. Who damns them to these tortures? *The God whom they have offended.* Who then is this God? *A God full of goodness.* But would a God full of goodness delight to bathe in their tears? Are these terrors not an insult against His forgiving nature? If criminals had to calm the furies of a tyrant, what more could they do?

VIII.

There are people who it would be improper to call "God-fearing": in reality, they're terrified of Him.

IX.

I am given a certain description of the Supreme Being, His bad temper, His vengeful rashness: the ratio of those He dispenses with to those he saves. From this portrait, an upright soul might be tempted to wish that He did not exist. We could really be at peace in this world if we were well assured that we had nothing to fear from the next one. The thought that there is no God has never frightened anyone; but rather that there is one, especially that one, is truly terrifying to many.

X.

We should not imagine that God is either too good or too wicked. Justice lies in the middle of the opposite extremes of clemency and cruelty; finite punishments are somewhere between license and eternal punishment.

XI.

I am aware that the shadier sides of superstition exist more in confession than in practice; that true believers don't really believe that they must hate themselves in order to love God, or live in poverty in order to be religious: their devotion is cheerful; their wisdom is very humane: but whence this difference in feeling from other people who bow to the same altars as themselves? Does piety also obey our blasted temperament? Well—how can you disagree? Its influence is only too plain in any given believer: his perceptions vary according to his affects; a vengeful God or a merciful one results; either hell or heaven will become his obsession: he shakes in fear, or he burns with love: it is a fever that can be hot or cold.

XII.

Yes, I maintain that superstition is more injurious to God than atheism is. "I would prefer," said Plutarch, "that Plutarch should never have existed, than to believe that Plutarch is unjust, full of rage, inconstant, jealous, and vindictive, and such that he would be happier not existing at all."

XIII.

Only a deist can go toe-to-toe with an atheist. The superstitious man lacks the required strength. His God is but an imaginary being. Aside from the difficulties of the matter, he is vulnerable to all the problems which result from the falsehood of his notions. Someone like Cudworth or Shaftesbury would have been a thousand times better stumbling-block for Vanini than all the Nicoles and Pascals in the world.

XIV.

Pascal was an upright fellow, but he was also timid and credulous. He was an elegant writer and a deep thinker, and he might have brought enlightenment to the world, had Providence not delivered him to certain people who sacrificed his great talents to their own prejudices. If only he had left the theologians of his day alone with their quarrels, if he had devoted himself wholly to the search for truth, without reservation or fear of offending God, taking advantage of all the gifts God gave him, and above all, if he had refused as his masters such men as were unworthy to be his disciples. We should apply to him what that clever man, La Mothe Le Vayer, said about Fontaine: that he was stupid enough to believe that

Arnauld, de Sacy and Nicole were more worthy than he was.

XV.

"I tell you that there is no God, that Creation is an illusion, that the eternal existence of the universe is no more disturbing than the eternal existence of the soul; that, because I can't imagine how movement was able to create this universe, which it somehow has the power to preserve, it is ridiculous to raise the specter of a Being who is even harder to imagine; that, if the wonders of the cosmos betray some intelligence at work, the disorders that reign in the moral order rule out any idea of a guiding Providence. I tell you that if everything is the handiwork of a God, then everything should be organized as well as possible: if everything is not the best that is possible, this shows that God is either less than all-powerful, or that He is not interested in the affair. Therefore, it is for the best that I am not more enlightened about His existence. That said, what do I have to do with your enlightenment? When you can plainly show me—which nobody has yet done—that every evil turns into something good: that it was great for Britannicus, the best of princes, to perish so that Nero, the worst of men, could reign; how then can you prove that it was not possible to attain the same end by other means? To allow vice, to better contrast against virtue, is to trade a very meager advantage for a very real disadvantage. There," said the atheist, "are my objections; what do you have to say? That I am a scoundrel? And that if I weren't afraid of God's judgment, I would not deny His existence?"

Let us leave this phrase to the orators: it may not be true; civility forbids it, and it shows little charity. Because a man goes wrong by denying God, is it right to insult him? People only resort to invective when they lack arguments. Take two people in any debate: odds are a hundred to one that the losing party will get upset. "You pick up your thunderbolts instead of responding to me," said Menippus to Jupiter. "This shows that you've lost the argument!"

XVI.

When asked one day whether there were any true atheists on Earth, a man responded: "Do you believe that there any true Christians?"

XVII.

All the metaphysical babble is not as powerful as a single argument *ad hominem.* In order to convince others, we must sometimes only stir up people's feelings, either physically or morally. At the business end of a baton, the greatest skeptic will find it hard to deny his own existence. That bandit Cartouche could have given Hobbes this kind of lesson, looking down the barrel of a pistol. "Your money or your life: there's nobody to help you, and I've got the upper hand; don't talk to *me* about justice."

XVIII.

The metaphysicians have been unable to take on atheism. All the sublime meditations of Malebranche and Descartes have done less to injure materialism than a single one of Malpighi's observations. If this dangerous hypothesis is tottering nowadays, this is due to the effects of experimental physics. It is only in the works of Newtown, Musschenbroek, Hartsoeker and Nieuwentyt that we have found satisfactory proofs of the existence of a supremely intelligent Being. Thanks to the labors of these great men, the world can no longer be seen as some kind of God: it is a machine with wheels, cords, pulleys, springs and weights.

XIX.

All the subtle arguments of ontology have only created skeptics, at best; but it is knowledge of nature that makes a true deist. The discovery of germs alone has dissolved one of the most powerful arguments for atheism. It does not matter whether movement is essential or incidental to matter; I am now convinced that its effects are limited to development: all empirical observations prove that putrefaction by itself can produce no new organism: I can allow that the mechanism of the simplest insect is no less marvelous than that of man; and I don't need to worry any longer that someone may infer that, if an internal agitation of molecules can lead to the creation of an insect, that it is likewise capable of making a man. If an atheist suggested two hundred years ago that we might one day see men springing full-grown from the bowels of the Earth, in the same way we sometimes see a swarm of insects emerge from a mass of heated flesh; I would love to know what arguments a metaphysician would have mustered back then.

XX.

It was always futile for me to try these scholastic subtleties on an atheist; the weakness of such arguments even gave him a sound objection: "A multitude of useless truths have been shown to me without any reply" he said, "but the existence of God, the reality of moral good and evil, and the immortality of the soul remain problematic for me; what then? Is it less important to be enlightened about these things, than to be convinced that the sum of the three angles of a triangle are equal to two right angles?"

An able speaker, he me made me drink his bitter thoughts deeply; I rose to the challenge with the sort of question that must have seemed bizarre to someone so puffed up with his initial victory:

"Are you a thinking being?" I asked him.

"How can you doubt that?" He replied with a self-satisfied

attitude.

"Why not doubt it? What convincing evidence do I have? A few sounds and movements? But a philosopher would notice the same features in an animal, and he denies that animals can think: why should I grant to you that which Descartes denied to the ants? You make convincing outward signs, and I feel tempted to believe that you really are thinking; but reason makes me suspend my judgment: 'There is no essential link between one's external acts and one's thoughts,' it tells me, 'and it is possible that your opponent here has no more thoughts than his pocket-watch does: should we assume the any animal we can teach to speak is also a thinking being? How do you know that people are anything more than well-trained parrots?'"

He replied: "that's a clever comparison; it is not only the movements and the sounds, but whether there is an organization of ideas, an understanding of the consequences that inhere within a chain of reasoning; that is how we judge whether a being has thoughts of its own: if I find a parakeet responding to a series of questions I might put to it, I would immediately grant it the status of a thinking being. But what does this question have to do with the existence of God? If you can prove to me that the smartest man I could name is actually an automaton, will I be better able to recognize intelligence in nature?"

"That's my own business," I replied. "For now, let's just agree that it would be madness to question the faculty of thought in your fellow humans."

"Okay, but what follows from that?"

"It follows that if the universe—but why do I say universe, when the mere wing of a butterfly offers me traces of an intelligence that are a thousand times more obvious than those that lead you to see intelligence in other people: it would be a thousand times more insane to deny the existence of a God than to deny that your fellow humans can think. But, be that as it may, let me speak directly to your intellect, to your very consciousness: have you not seen in the reasoning, actions and behavior of any given person more intelligence, order, wisdom, and systematic procedure than in the mechanism of an insect? Is the Divinity not as clearly discernible in the eye of a mite, as a man's faculty of thinking is in the works of great Newton? What? Does the world, fashioned as we find it, demonstrate intelligence any less than the world as explained to us by some man? What a strange idea!"

"Come on, I grant the ability of thinking in another, even more willingly than in myself."

Fine, I agree, that's a presumption I didn't have: but I have the consolation that my arguments are better than yours. Is not the intelligence of a first Being better demonstrated by nature: that is, by His workmanship, than the faculty of thinking in a philosopher is by his writings? Note that I have only waved the wing of a butterfly at you, and shown you the eye of a mite, when I could have crushed you with the weight of the whole universe. Either I am greatly mistaken, or this proof is better even than what has been taught in the universities. It is on this rationale, and some others, equally simple, that I base my belief in the existence of God, and not on those tissues of dry and metaphysical ideas which obscure the truth more than they clarify anything.

XXI.

I open the notebook of a famous professor, and I read: "Dear atheists, I grant you that movement is part of the essence of matter; but what do you conclude from this? ...That the world came from the random combination of atoms? Why not say that Homer's *Iliad* or Voltaire's *Henriade* could likewise come into existence through a random combination of letters?" Now, I would be cautious about using this argument on an atheist, because it would only give him a chance to have some fun at your expense:

"According to the laws of probability," he would respond, "we should expect that if something is possible, it will happen. The low likelihood of the event you describe is balanced by the multitude of chances to bring it about. There are a certain number of times I might roll a hundred thousand sixes, using a hundred thousand dice. However unlikely it is that the letters should come together by random chance to compose *The Iliad*, given enough chances, it becomes possible: I would have an infinitely good chance of victory, if the quantity of chances were agreed to be infinite. So you'll really grant me," he would persist, "that matter exists from all eternity, and that movement is part of its essence? To return the favor, I will grant you that the universe has no boundaries, that there are an infinity of atoms, and that this order, which astonishes you so much, never breaks down anywhere. But, from these reciprocal views, nothing follows except the fact that the possibility of bringing the universe about by chance is remote; but the number of chances is infinite, that is to say, that the improbability of its happening is more than sufficiently compensated by the number of chances. Therefore if anything here is contrary to reason, it is the claim that matter has been in motion from all eternity, and that in the infinite sum of possible combinations, perhaps an infinite number of good arrangements are possible; however, among the infinite number of forms it has assumed from all eternity, none of these good arrangements were ever retained. Therefore, the human mind should be astonished more at the hypothetical duration of chaos, than at the fact that the universe should have taken shape at some point."

XXII.

As far as I'm concerned, there are three kinds of atheists. There are some who will frankly tell you that there is no God, and who think the same thing: *these are the true atheists.* Then there are quite a few who do not know what to think about it, and who would resolve the matter with the toss of a coin; *these are the skeptical atheists.* There are many more who prefer that God shouldn't exist, and who make a great show of being persuaded in this opinion, and who live as if it were true; *these are the sect's windbags.* I can't stand the last of these, for they are false: I pity the true atheists, for all consolation would seem to be unavailable to them; and I pray to God for the skeptics, for they lack understanding.

XXIII.

Deists believe in God, the immortality of the soul and its consequences; skeptics are uncertain on these issues, while atheists deny both. Therefore, skeptics have one motive more than the atheists to be virtuous, and fewer than deists. Without fear of the Lawgiver, benevolence, or awareness of virtue's advantages in this life, the morality of atheists lacks a firm basis, and that of the skeptic is founded on a "perhaps."

XXIV.

Skepticism is not for everyone. It presupposes thorough and disinterested examination: he who doubts because he is unacquainted with the arguments for belief, is but an ignoramus. The true skeptic has found and weighed up these arguments. But this is no small matter. Who among us knows exactly how to weight each argument? Even if you bring out a hundred proofs for a single dogma, none of them will lack for partisans. Every mind sees through its own set of lenses. An argument that seems colossal to me may be minor to you; a question that crushes me may strike you as frivolous. If we are divided on their value individually, how can we agree on their relative weights? Do tell, how many moral proofs should I balance against a metaphysical conclusion? Are my glasses out of focus, or yours? If it's this hard to weigh up the reasons, and if these questions have supporters on every side, who nearly always balance each other out, then why do we cut each other off so quickly? Why use such a confident tone? Have we not felt repulsed countless times by the self-satisfied attitude of dogmatist? Montaigne, in his Essays (Book 3, chapter 11) said that "when people try to make me think that certain things are beyond dispute; this makes me dislike them, even when they do seem probable. I love those words that soften and moderate the temerity of our propositions, like 'perhaps', 'not at all', 'sometimes", 'it is said', 'I think', and such like; if I had children to teach, I would assume a questing and unresolved tone, using words like: 'that is to say', 'I do not understand that', 'that may be', 'is it true?'; I would rather have them acting like pupils until the age of sixty, than carry on like doctors at the age of ten."

XXV.

What is God? We put this question to children, and the philosophers have a hard time with it.

We know the appropriate age for a child to learn to read, to sing or dance, to learn Latin, or to take up geometry. But when it comes to religion, we pay no attention to this concern: the child is hardly out of the womb when we start to ask it the question, "What is God?" And in the same period, from the same mouth he learns about goblins, ghosts, werewolves, and God. We inculcate one of the most important truths in such a way that it can be falsified at the bar of reason in later life. Why are we surprised to find that since the existence of God is jumbled up in his head with a host of ridiculous prejudices, and by the time he's twenty he starts to misunderstand God and treat Him the way our judges treat a man who was in the wrong time and place, and was swept up and arrested along with a gang of thugs?

XXVI.

We learn about God too early; another failing is that we do not emphasize His presence very much. We have banished God; we have relegated Him to a sanctuary; the walls of a temple hide Him from sight; He doesn't exist outside of it. O madman that you are, break down these walls that hold your ideas in, and magnify God: you will see Him in every place where He is, or say that He is nowhere. If I had a child to educate, I would portray God as so real a companion that for him to become an atheist would cost him no less than the loss of His companionship. Instead of pointing to the good example of some other fellow, who may not deserve this pedestal, I would roughly tell him, "God is listening, and you're fibbing." The young require sense impressions; I would therefore multiply around him all manner of signs pointing to the presence of the Divinity. If, for example, we held a gathering, I would indicate where God's place was, and I would get him used to saying, "There were four of us: God, my friend, my tutor and myself."

XXVII.

Ignorance and incuriosity are two very soft pillows, but to find them so, our head must be as well-made as Montaigne's (*Essays* book 3, chapter 8).

XXVIII.

A vigorous mind and an ardent imagination don't agree with the indolence of the skeptic. People like that prefer to run a great risk than take no chance at all: to be mistaken rather than live in uncertainty; either uncertain of the strength in their arms, or nervous about the depth of the waters, we always see them dangling from branches they know are feeble, but they would rather hang on than drop into the torrent. They believe everything, although they have not examined anything carefully: they doubt nothing, since they lack due patience and courage. Relying entirely on glimmering lights, if by chance they find the truth, it is not by groping along in the dark, but suddenly, as if by revelation. Among those of the dogmatic persuasion, they are what the illuminati are among the pietists.

I have seen people like this become distraught when they failed to imagine how a person could live in mental tranquility in the midst of indecision: "How can you be happy when you don't know what we are, where we come from, where we are going, or why we are here?"

"I'm not happy about not knowing all these things, but I don't let it get to me," the skeptic responded flatly. "It's not my fault if I've found judgment to be mute just when I needed its guidance most. All my life I have been unaware of everything that was impossible to know, but I don't let it get me down. Why should I feel bad about failing to know something which can't, after all, be all that important to know? 'Should I,' asked one of the first geniuses of our age, 'really be upset that I don't have four eyes, four feet, and two wings?'"

XXIX.

I must strive after the truth, but I'm under no obligation to find it in the end. Is it not true that a piece of sophistry can affect me more powerfully than a solid proof? I must consent to the false belief that I mistake for a true one, and reject the true one which I take to be false: but what have I to fear if I am mistaken in good faith? We cannot find a reward in another world for having been clever in this one; therefore, shall we be punished for having been less intelligent? To damn a man for following bad logic is to forget that he's only an idiot and to judge him as wicked instead.

XXX.

What is a skeptic? It is a philosopher who has doubted everything that he believes, and who believes whatever the legitimate use of his reason and sense perception have revealed to be true. Need I clarify further? Make the Pyrrhonist sincere, and you will have your skeptic.

XXXI.

If something has never been questioned, it has never been demonstrated. That which has never been examined without hindrance has never been fully examined. Skepticism, then, is the first step towards truth. It should be universalized, for it is the touchstone of truth. If, by way of assuring himself of God's existence, the philosopher begins by doubting it, is any idea beyond challenge?

XXXII.

Unbelief is sometimes the vice of an idiot, and credulity the failing of an intelligent man. The wise man sees far into the immense depth of possibilities; the idiot fails to imagine any possibilities outside of what already is. That is perhaps what makes the one quarrelsome, and the other reckless.

XXXIII.

We risk as much by believing too much as we do by believing too little. There is neither more nor less danger in being a polytheist or an atheist; yet skepticism alone can be equally spared, at all times, and in all places, from these two extremes.

XXXIV.

A half-hearted skepticism is the mark of a weak mind; it reveals an argumentative thinker, afraid of where his reason leads; a superstitious man who believes he honors his God by the constraints he places on his reason; a kind of unbeliever who is afraid that others will see through him: for if the truth has nothing to fear from examination, as this semi-skeptic is convinced, what does he think at the bottom of his heart about those privileged notions that he learns to discover, which he tucks away on a certain shelf in his head, in a sanctuary he does not dare approach?

XXXV.

I hear accusations of infidelity all around. The Christian is an infidel in Asia; same goes for the Muslim in Europe, the Catholic in London, the Calvinist in Paris, the Jansenist at the top of the rue Saint-Jacques, the Molinist in the suburb of Saint-Médard. Who, then, is an infidel? Everyone, or no-one?

XXXVI.

When believers argue against skepticism, I think that they misunderstand their own self-interest, or they are inconsistent. If it is true that all it takes for a true religion to be embraced, and for a false one to be abandoned, is for them to be properly understood, then it would be a great thing for universal doubt to spread across the globe, and to have everyone question their own religion: our missionaries would find the job half-done already.

XXXVII.

He who does not stay in the religion he was raised in, can no more glory in being a Christian or Muslim, than he can of not being born blind or lame. It is good fortune, and is not due to merit.

XXXVIII.

He who dies for a religion that he knows to be false is insane.

He who dies for a false religion, which he believes in, or for a true religion which he has no good reason to believe in, is a fanatic. The true martyr is he who dies for a true religion, the truth of which he is sure of.

XXXIX.

The true martyr waits for death to come to him, whereas the fanatic runs towards it.

XL.

If someone went to Mecca, walked right up to Muhammad's ashes and spat on them, overturning his altars and upsetting a whole Mosque, he would find himself at the end of a blade straight away, and he would be unlikely to be granted sainthood for his trouble. This kind of zeal is out of fashion. Polyeuctus would be taken for a madman nowadays.

XLI.

Revelations, miracles, and extraordinary missions have had their day. Christianity has no further need of this kind of scaffolding. If a man should follow in Jonah's footsteps, running through the streets crying: "Yet three days, and Paris will be no more: Parisians, repent in sackcloth and ashes, or in three days you shall perish!" such a man would be immediately bound and brought before a judge, who would consign him to the nearest asylum. He may be right to say, "O people, does God love you less than the Ninevites? Are you any less guilty than they were?" We would waste no effort by responding to this; and, treating him as delusional, we would pay no attention to his deadline.

Elijah can come back from the other world whenever he likes; the way people are now, it would be a great miracle indeed if he got a good reception in this one.

XLII.

When someone publicly proclaims a teaching which contradicts the dominant religion, or any teachings that threaten public tranquility, perhaps confirming their mission by miracles, then the government can rightfully crack down, and the people are allowed to shout: "Crucify him!" To leave the people to chase after the seductions of an impostor, or the dreams of a delusional man, is irresponsible governance. If the blood of Jesus Christ had called vengeance upon the Jews, it is because by spilling it they shut their ears to the voices of Moses and the Prophets, who predicted the Messiah. Should an angel come down from heaven, supporting his words with miracles, and yet if he proclaims anything against the law of Jesus Christ, Paul wants us to call him anathema. Thus it is not by miracles that we should judge the mission of a man, but by the conformity of his doctrine with that of the people to whom he is sent, above all when the doctrine of the people is demonstrably true.

XLIII.

All innovation in government is dangerous. The holiest religion and best one, Christianity itself, was not established without causing certain disturbances. The first children of the Church more than once departed from the moderation and patience which had been enjoined them. I will share some excerpts from an edict of Emperor Julian; they reveal the genius of this philosopher-king, and the attitude of the zealots of his day:

"I expected that the leaders of the Galileans would sense how different my policy was from that of my predecessor, and that they would feel some gratitude: under his reign they suffered exile and prisons; a multitude of those whom they call heretics were put to the sword... Under my reign, we have called back the exiles, liberated the prisoners, and redeemed the property of others. But such is the noisy fury of these people, that since they lost the privilege of devouring each other, of torturing both those who are attached to their own beliefs, and those who follow the religion authorized by the laws, they spare no means, nor miss any opportunity to stir up trouble; people without regard for true piety, and without respect for our ordinances... We do not hear that anyone is dragged before our altars, nor of any violence done to them... As for the masses, it appears that their leaders stir up the spirit of sedition in them; they are furious about the bounds we set to their ambitions; for we have excluded them from our tribunals, and they have lost the convenience of disposing of testaments, of supplanting legitimate heirs, or seizing inheritances... This is why we forbid them from assembling in a tumult and forming conspiracies with seditious priests... May this edict ensure the security of our magistrates whom this mutinous people has insulted more than once, and placed in danger of being stoned... They can peaceably meet with their leaders at their places of worship, they can pray there, and receive instruction, there they can worship in their own way, and this is authorized: but they must renounce all seditious conspiracies... And if these assemblies are abused to organize a revolt, it will be at the risk of their lives and fortunes, let them beware... O unbelieving people, please live in peace... And you who remain faithful to the religion of your country and to the gods of your fathers, do not persecute your neighbors, your fellow citizens, whose ignorance is more to be pitied than their wickedness is to be blamed... It is by reason and not violence that we will lead men back to truth. We enjoin you then, our faithful subjects, to leave the Galileans in peace."

Such were the sentiments of that ruler. Fault him for being a pagan if you like, but not an apostate: he spent the first years of his life under several tutors and in various schools; when he came of age, made an unfortunate choice: sadly, he opted for his ancestral religion, and the gods of his native land.

XLIV.

What astonishes me is the fact that the writings of this wise emperor have survived for us to read them. Some of what he wrote, while by no means doing harm to the truth of Christianity, is so defamatory to certain Christians of his day that it would have drawn the particular attentions of the Church Fathers, who were very eager to suppress the writings of their enemies. It was apparently from his predecessors that Saint Gregory the Great inherited that barbarous zeal which animated him against literature and the arts. If it were up to that pontiff, we would be like the Muslims, who are only allowed to read the Qur'an. For, what would have become of the ancient writers in the hands of a man who abused language on principle, who thought that obedience to grammar was to subject Jesus Christ to grammarians like Donatus, and who thought that conscience compelled him to erase every trace of the ruins of antiquity?

XLV.

However, the divinity of the Scriptures is not so clearly imprinted in them that the authority of the sacred historians can stand on its own two feet, independent of the profane writers. Where would we be if we had to recognize the finger of God in the form our Bible has taken! The Latin version is despicable! Even the originals are far from masterpieces of composition. The prophets, the apostles and evangelists wrote according to their own understanding. If we may read the histories of the Hebrew people simply as a production of the human mind, Moses and his successors would not surpass Titus Livius, Sallust, Caesar, or Josephus, none of whom claimed to have written under divine inspiration. Do we not prefer even that Jesuit Berruyer to Moses?

In our churches we preserve paintings which we are told were painted by angels and even by God Himself: if the same works had come from the hands of Le Sueur or Le Brun, what criticism could I lay at the feet of this timeless tradition? Nothing, probably. But when I observe these heavenly works, and I see all the rules of painting being violated in their design and execution; everything that is true in art is everywhere discarded. Since I can't suppose that the artist was ignorant of such things, I must expect that these are falsifications.

I might draw an analogy to the Holy Scriptures, did I not know how little it matters whether what they say is well-said or badly stated. Were the prophets not concerned the truth, rather than eloquence? Did the apostles die for anything more than the truths they preached or wrote? Yet, to return to the point at hand, would it not have been important to preserve the writings of the profane authors, who could not fail to agree with the sacred authors, at least on the existence and the miracles of Jesus Christ, on the qualities and character of Pontius Pilate, and on the deeds and martyrdom of the first Christians?

XLVI.

A whole people, you tell me, witnessed this miracle: do you really dare to deny it? Yes, I dare, unless you can find an independent and unimpeachable witness for me. Moreover, if an allegedly impartial writer mentioned that a gulf opened up in the middle of a city; that the gods who were consulted answered that it would close up again once the city's most precious possession was thrown in, and that when a brave knight was dropped in, the prophecy was fulfilled, I would be less inclined to believe him than if he said that a gulf opened up and considerable time and efforts were required to fill it again. The less plausible a fact seems, the more the historical evidence loses its force. I would easily believe a single honest man who announced that "His Majesty has just won a total victory over the allies", but if every person in Paris assured me that a dead man was resurrected in Passy, I would have none of it. That a historian should impose on us, or that a whole people should be mistaken, are hardly novelties.

XLVII.

Tarquin made plans to augment the cavalry which Romulus had formed. An augur stood against his plans, maintaining that any innovation in the military is sacrilege, unless accompanied by a divine mandate. Shocked by this priest's manner, and having resolved to set up for public ridicule both this man and an art which checked his authority, Tarquin called him to the public square, and challenged him: "Soothsayer, tell me, is it possible to do what I am thinking of? If your knowledge matches your boast, you will have the answer." The augur consulted his birds and responded calmly: "Yes, prince, what you contemplate can indeed be done." So Tarquin pulled a razor from his robe, and taking a stone in his hand, said, "Approach, tell the soothsayer to slice this stone with this razor; for I had been contemplating whether this was possible." Navius (this was the augur's name) turned to the people and said confidently, "Set the razor to the stone, and haul me off to the dungeons if the stone is not sliced in half before your eyes." It happened just as he had said; the stone gave way to the razor's edge: it split so quickly that the razor cut into Tarquin's hand and drew blood. The people, astonished, shouted praise; Tarquin relented and declared himself the protector of the augurs; the razor and stone's halves were preserved in an altar; a statue was erected in memory of the diviner: it remained in place even to the reign of Augustus; profane and sacred antiquity both attest to the truth of this fact: it can be found in Lactantius, Denis of Halicarnassus, and Saint Augustine.

You've heard the story; now hear the superstition:

"What do you say about that?" The superstitious Quintus asked his brother Cicero. "We must fall into a monstrous skepticism, regard the people and historians as idiots and burn the chronicles, or we must agree that it really happened. Will you deny everything rather than agree that the gods intervene in our affairs?"

"Then dismiss Romulus's augural staff, which you say the hottest of fires was powerless to burn, and attach slight importance to the whetstone of Attus Navius. Myths would have no place in philosophy. It would have been more in keeping with your role as a philosopher to consider, first, the nature of divination generally, second, its origin, and third, its consistency. What, then, is the nature of an art which makes prophets out of birds that wander aimlessly about — now here, now there — and makes the action or inaction of men depend upon the song or flight of birds? and why was the power granted to some birds to give a favorable omen when on the left side and to others when on the right? Again, however, when, and by whom, shall we say that the system was invented? The Etruscans, it is true, find the author of their system in the boy who was ploughed up out of the ground; but whom have we? Attus Navius?"

"But this is the same thing that is accepted by Kings, peoples, nations and everyone else."

"As if there were anything as absolutely common as want of sense, or as if you yourself in deciding anything would accept the opinion of the mob?"[3] That's how the philosopher responded. Now, name a single miracle to which this would not equally be applicable! The Church Fathers, who doubtless saw the great difficulties inherent in following Cicero's principles, preferred to allow the truthfulness of the story of Tarquin, and to attribute the art of Navius to the devil. What a handy tool the devil can be.

XLVIII.

All nations have certain wonder-stories whose only fault is that they are not true: by means of these anything can be

---

[3] Cicero, *On Divination*, Book 2, chaps. 80, 81 – Translation from the Loeb edition.

demonstrated, but nothing can be proved; they cannot be denied without impiety, but they cannot be believed without imbecility.

XLIX.

Romulus, having either been struck by lightning or murdered by the senators, one way or another he disappeared from among the Romans. The people and the army murmured about it. The orders in the state engaged in mutual conflict; young Rome, divided from within, and surrounded by enemies without, was, as it were, on the edge of a cliff when a certain Proculeius solemnly came forward and said: "Romans, this ruler, whose loss you feel so keenly, is not dead at all: he went up to Heaven, where he sits on the right hand of Jupiter.' Go on,' he told me, "and relieve your fellow citizens: tell them that Romulus is with the Gods: reassure them of my protection: let them know that the powers of their enemies will never defeat them: destiny decrees that they will one day rule the world: may they hand this prophecy down from age to age, until their furthest descendants.'"

Sometimes imposture is favored by circumstances, and if we examine the state of affairs of Rome at the time, we must concur that Proculeius was a clever fellow who knew an opportunity when he saw one. He introduced a prejudice which turned out to be quite beneficial for the future greatness of his homeland... "It was strange how the man who announced these tidings was believed, and how the people's longing for Romulus was satisfied when they came to believe in his immortality. Admiration of the hero and fear embellished the story; little by little, Romulus became hailed as a god, and the son of a god, by all." That is to say, the People believed in this apparition; the Senators made a show of believing it and altars were raised to Romulus. But things did not stay that way. It was not long before Romulus made additional post-mortem visits: he showed himself to a thousand people in a day. Lightning had not struck Romulus;

the Senators had not done away with him under cover of a heavy storm: no, he ascended into the air amid the bolts of lightning and peals of thunder, as witnessed by all; this story was gradually embellished with many additions which must have embarrassed the sharper wits of succeeding ages.

L.

A single demonstration strikes me more than fifty deeds. Thanks to the extreme confidence I have in my reason, my faith is safe from attack. Pontiff of Muhammad, make the lame walk! Give speech to the dumb! Give sight to the blind! Heal the paralytics! Revive the dead; even restore missing limbs to the maimed (a miracle not yet attempted), and to your great astonishment my faith will not be shaken. Do you want me to convert? Then set aside your miracles, and let us talk. I have more confidence in my judgment than in my eyes.

If the religion you proclaim is true, its truth can be shown and demonstrated by invincible reasoning. So find out these reasons. Why harass me by miracles, when all it takes to floor me is a syllogism? What then—could it actually be easier to heal the lame than to enlighten me?

LI.

A man is stretched out on the ground, without sensation, making no sound, with no body heat, not moving at all. We roll him around, shake him, prod him with flame, but nothing makes him move: hot irons cannot draw any signs of life from him; we believe he is dead: so is he or not? No. It is the priest of Calama, "who, when he pleased, distanced himself from all feeling and lay like a corpse, so that he did not feel those who pinched and pricked him, and was even quite unaware of being burnt by fire, save for the after-effect."[4] If certain people

---

[4] Saint Augustine, City of God, Book 14, Chap. 24.

came across a similar case in our times, they would have put his talents to use. We would see a cadaver reanimated by the ashes of a saint; the collection of miracle-stories by a certain Jansenist magistrate would have swollen by the addition of a resurrection, and the Constitutionalists would perhaps have been confounded.

LII.

We must agree, says the logician of Port-Royal, that Saint Augustine was right to sustain, with Plato, that the judgment of truth and the rules for discerning it do not belong to the senses, but to the mind: *Non est veritatis judicum in sensibus*[5]. Even this sense-certainty is not very extensive, and we think we know many things by their mediation, which we are not truly certain about. So, when the testimony of the senses contradicts or does not counterbalance the authority of reason, we have no choice: logically, we must cling to reason.

LIII.

A certain street is full of shouts of joy: there, in a single day, the ashes of a saint once performed more miracles than Jesus Christ did in his whole life. People are running there, on foot or carried along by the mob; I follow the crowd. When I finally arrive, I hear cries of: "It's a miracle! A miracle!" I approach, I look, and I see a small cripple parading about with three or four charitable people who hold him up; and the people are marveling, repeating: "It's a miracle, a miracle!" So where is your miracle, O idiotic mob? Don't you see that this child has only exchanged one set of crutches for another? On this occasion there were in fact miracles, as it ever was, in the minds of the people. I take it for certain that everyone who has seen a ghost was already terrified that they would see one, and that everyone who saw miracles there had made up their

---

[5] There is no truth in the judgment of the senses.

minds beforehand about seeing one.

LIV.

We have, nevertheless, a large tome before us which describes enough apparent miracles to crush the most ardent skeptic. Its author is a senator, a serious man who once professed, let's be honest, a poorly-grasped materialism, but he didn't even wait for his conversion to make his fortune. He was an eyewitness of the facts he relates, of which he has been able to judge without prejudice or bias, and to his own testimony he has added countless others. They all say what they saw, and their depositions have all possible authenticity: the originals are preserved in the public archives. What do you say now? What do you say? *That miracles prove nothing, unless a person has already made up their mind.*

LV.

Any argument that works for both sides in a dispute is useless. Fanaticism has its martyrs, just like the true religion, and among those who died for the true religion, even some of them were fanatics; let's tally our respective cadavers, if possible, and then choose which side to believe—otherwise let us seek other reasons for belief.

LVI.

Nothing is better at shoring up irreligion than false motives for conversion. Unbelievers are always told: "Who are you to attack a religion which was so courageously defended by Paul, Tertullian, Athanasius, Chrysostom, Augustine, Cyprian, and many other famous people? So, you've come across some difficulty that these intellects have overlooked! Prove that you're smarter than all of them, or, if you agree with their intellectual superiority, then give up your doubts!" What a frivolous argument. The intelligence of its ministers in no way proves the veracity of a religion. What sect was more absurd than that of the Egyptians, but what religion ever had a more enlightened clergy than that one?

...“No, I won't worship this onion. What makes it better than the rest of the plant kingdom? I'd be an idiot to sing hymns to something that's going to end up in my belly! What fine god to have—a plant that I myself planted, one that grew and died in my own pot!"

"Silence, you wretch, your blasphemies make me tremble! Who are you to argue with us? Do you think you know more than the Holy Order? Who are you to attack the gods, to counsel its ministers? Are you more enlightened than the oracles, to which everyone on Earth comes for guidance? Say what you will, your pride or temerity are horrendous..."

Do Christians never feel all their power, and will they never abandon these unfortunate sophisms to such as have them as their only resort? "Let us omit anything that can be said on both sides, though they cannot truly be said to be on both sides"[6]. Example, miracles, and authority can make people either dupes or hypocrites: reason alone makes them into believers.

LVII.

It is generally agreed that it is of ultimate importance only to use sturdy reasoning in defense of the faith; but it's also common for those who expose bad reasoning to suffer persecution—but why? Is it not enough that we should be Christians? Must we also be Christians for bad reasons? You devout ones, take note: I am not a Christian because Saint Augustine was one; but because it is reasonable to be one.

---

[6] Saint Augustine, *City of God*.

LVIII.

I know the devout, and they are quick to raise the alarm. If they decide that this book contains something that against their ideas, I expect the same sort of slander that they have smeared across the names of countless more capable writers than me. If I am only called a deist and a wicked man, I'll be doing pretty well. They damned Descartes, Montaigne, Locke, and Bayle, and I expect they will damn many others as well. I declare, however, than I am happy to be no more honest a man, and no better a Christian, than most of the philosophers.

I was born into the Catholic, Apostolic and Roman Church, and I subject myself completely to all of its decisions. I want to die in this, my ancestral religion, and I believe it is good, as far as such a thing is possible for someone who has never had any immediate dealings with the Divinity, nor ever witnessed any miracle.

There you have my confession of faith: I am almost certain that it will fail to satisfy them, although I expect that not one of them could sincerely confess a better one.

LIX.

I have had occasion to read Abbadie, Huet, and the rest of them. I know the proofs of my religion well enough, and I agree that they're fantastic; but should they be a hundred times better, still Christianity would not have been proved true. Why then demand that I believe that there are three persons in God, as firmly as I believe that the sum of three angles of a triangle are equal to two right angles. Any proof should produce in me a certainty proportional to its strength; the effect of geometrical, moral and physical demonstrations on my mind should all be different, otherwise this distinction is frivolous.

LX.

You hand a volume of Scripture to an unbeliever, the divinity of which you claim to demonstrate to him. But before entering into his examination of your proofs, he won't fail to ask you something about this collection:

"Has it always been the same?" he will ask you. "Why is the collection smaller now than it was in former ages? What right had someone to remove this book which one sect revered, and preserve this other one which another sect rejected? On what basis have you preferred this manuscript to others? Who directed you in the choice between so many different copies, which is a clear indication that the sacred authors were not transmitted in their primitive purity?

"But if the ignorance of copyists or the malice of heretics has corrupted them, as you must allow, you see that you must first restore them to their native state before you try to prove their divinity, for you'll get nowhere by promoting this collection of mutilated tatters. But, who will you trust to carry out this necessary restoration? The Church. But I can't agree with you about the infallibility of the Church until you prove the divinity of the Scriptures. So you see how I necessarily fall into skepticism."

The only way to respond to this problem is by affirming that the first foundations of the Faith are purely human; that the choice between manuscripts, the restitution of certain passages, and the collection itself was created according to rules of criticism; I am happy to grant a degree of faith in the divinity of the sacred books in proportion to the certainty of these rules.

LXI.

The books that contain the grounds for my belief also present reasons for incredulity. The same arsenal is available to both sides in this battle: with the very same books, I have seen the deist arm himself against the atheist; the deist and the atheist warring against the Jew; the atheist, the deist and the Jew making common cause against the Christian; the Christian, the Jew, the deist, and the atheist joining forces against the Muslim; the atheist, the deist, the Jew, the Muslim, and diverse Christian sects making war on the Christian—each laying into the other, and the skeptic alone against all. I was the referee, holding the balance between the combatants, its arms raised or lowered by the weights they carried. After long oscillations, things seemed to be going best for the Christian, but this was due only to his numbers. I can bear witness of my impartiality, but this victory did not appear very great to me. God is my witness.

LXII.

This diversity of opinions has made the deists imagine an argument that is perhaps more unique than it is sound. When Cicero set out to show that the Romans were the most belligerent people on Earth, he cleverly drew this affirmation from the mouths of their enemies:

"Gauls, to whom if any, do you yield in courage? To the Romans. Parthians, after you, who are the most courageous men? The Romans. Africans, whom would you fear, if you were to fear anyone? The Romans."

The deists say, "let us, following his example, interrogate each of the religions: Chinese, what religion would be best, if not your own? Natural religion. Muslims, what faith would you embrace, should you ever swear off Muhammad? Naturalism. Christians, which is the true religion, if it is not Christianity? The religion of the Jews. But you, O Jews, which is the true religion, if Judaism is false? Naturalism."

"Now those," Cicero continues, "who are awarded second place unanimously, and who do not in turn yield first place to anyone deserve, without contest, first place."

ADDITION TO THE "PHILOSOPHICAL THOUGHTS"

1770

I.

Rather than impiety, religious doubts should be seen as good works, provided they occur to a man who humbly recognizes his ignorance, and when these doubts come from the fear of displeasing God by abusing reason.

II.

To admit that there is some conformity between the reason that is in man and the eternal reason which is God, and then to claim that God demands the sacrifice of human reason, is to say that He simultaneously wants and does not want something.

III.

If God, who gave us the gift of reason, also demands that we sacrifice it, then He's a swindler who steals back what he gave you.

IV.

If I renounce my reason I give up my only guide: I would then have to blindly adopt some secondary principle, and presuppose the very thing that is in dispute.

V.

If reason is a gift from Heaven, and if the same can be said of faith, then Heaven has given us a pair of incompatible and contradictory gifts.

VI.

To escape this impasse, we must say that faith is an illusory principle, and that it does not exist in nature.

VII.

Pascal, Nicole, and others have said: "The fact that a God punishes, by eternal judgments, the fault of a guilty parent on every one of his innocent children, is a proposition that is superior to, and not contrary to, reason." But then what proposition could possibly be contrary to reason, if not one which openly blasphemes against God?

VIII.

Lost in an immense forest at night, I have but a small light to guide me. A stranger appears and tells me: "My friend, blow out your candle, the better to find your path." This stranger is a theologian.

IX.

If my reason comes from on high, then the voice of Heaven speaks to me by this means; I must listen.

X.

Merit and demerit cannot be applied to the use of reason: all the good will in the world can avail nothing to help a blind man discern colors. I am compelled to see the evidence wherever it lies, and the lack of evidence where it is absent, provided I'm no imbecile; yet imbecility is a misfortune and not a vice.

XI.

The author of nature, who will not reward me for having been clever, will not damn me for being an idiot.

XII.

Nor will He damn you even for having been wicked. Why not? Is a wicked life in itself not punishment enough?

XIII.

All virtuous behavior produces internal satisfaction, and misdeeds remorse; yet the mind is repulsed by certain ideas without any shame: so there is neither virtue nor crime either in believing or in rejecting them.

XIV.

If still further grace is required for us to do what is right, then what was the death of Jesus Christ for?

XV.

If a hundred thousand are damned per each soul that is saved, then the devil has always been ahead in the game, and he didn't even have to put his own son to death.

XVI.

The Christian God is a father who dotes on his apples but neglects his children.

XVII.

Take away a Christian's fear of Hell, and his whole belief structure will collapse.

XVIII.

A true religion, involving all men in all times and in all places, should be eternal, universal and obvious; none of them have these three characteristics. All are then proven false three times over.

XIX.

Any facts which only certain men can witness are not adequate to verify a religion which is to be equally believed by everyone.

XX.

The facts by which the religions are supported are both ancient and miraculous: that is to say, things which are as doubtful as possible are used to prove what is least credible of all.

XXI.

To prove the Gospel by means of a miracle is to prove an absurdity by something that is against nature.

XXII.

But what shall God do to those who never heard the proclamation of His Son? Will He punish the deaf for failing to listen?

XXIII.

What will He do to those who have been told about His religion, but were unable to understand it? Would He punish a pygmy if he can't walk in a giant's tracks?

XXIV.

Why are the miracles of Jesus Christ true, but those done by Aesculapius, Apollonius of Tyana and Muhammad are false?

XXV.

But weren't all the Jews who were in Jerusalem converted by witnessing the miracles of Jesus Christ? No, by no means. Far from believing in him, they crucified him. We would have to consider these Jews as truly unique in history; everywhere else, people get led away by a single false miracle, while Jesus Christ was unable to get anywhere with the Jewish people in spite of an endless train of true miracles.

XXVI.

It is this miracle of the Jewish incredulity that really deserves the emphasis, not the miracle of the resurrection.

XXVII.

It's as sure as that two and two make four that Caesar existed; it is equally certain that Jesus Christ existed like Caesar...therefore, it is equally certain that Jesus Christ was resurrected, as it is that he or Caesar existed.

What a piece of logic! The mere existence of Jesus Christ and Caesar are not miracles.

XXVIII.

We read in the biography of Mr. De Turenne that once, when fire broke out in a certain house, the presence of the Holy Sacrament suddenly stopped its progress. Fair enough. But we also read in the same book that when a monk poisoned a consecrated host, a German emperor had no sooner swallowed it than he died from it.

XXIX.

Either it contained something other than the appearance of bread and water, or we must conclude that poison was incorporated to the body and blood of Jesus Christ.

XXX.

This body collects mold, this blood turns sour. Such a God is devoured by mites upon his altar. Blind masses, stupid Egyptian, open your eyes!

XXXI.

The religion of Jesus Christ, as proclaimed by ignorant men, created the first Christians. The same religion, as preached by learned men and doctors, creates nothing today but unbelievers.

XXXII.

It is objected that submission to a legislative authority does away with reason. But where is there, on the face of the Earth, any religion without such an authority?

XXXIII.

It is education from the crib onwards that keeps a Muslim from being baptized; education from the crib onwards is what keeps a Christian from getting himself circumcised; but it is the rationality of the grown man that leads him to despise both baptism and circumcision equally.

XXXIV.

In Luke's gospel it is said that God the Father is greater than God the son: *pater major me est* ("the Father is greater than me"). Meanwhile the Church, which can't stand such plain language, pronounces anathemas on any of the faithful who are so scrupulous as to take the words of the Testament of their Father so literally.

XXXV.

If authority has been able to dispose of this passage as it pleases, which is as plain as anything in the Bible, there is not a single passage that we can flatter ourselves of having properly understood, and with which the Church may not in the future do whatever it likes.

XXXVI.

Tu es petrus, et super hunc petram aedificabo ecclesiam meam ("Thou art Peter, and on this Rock I will build my Church"). Is this the language of a God, or a clever line worthy of our rhymester Seigneur des Accords?

XXXVII.

In dolore paries ("You will give birth in pain"), said God to the erring woman. But what did the female animals do to offend him, since they also suffer when they give birth?

XXXVIII.

If we take Jesus' statement: *Pater major me est:* ("the Father is greater than me") literally, then Jesus Christ is not God. If we understand this one literally: *Hoc est corpus meum* ("this is my body"), he gave himself to his apostles with his own hands, which is as absurd as to say that Saint Dennis held and lowered his own head after it had been hacked off.

XXXIX.

It is said that he retired to the Mount of Olives, and that he prayed. And to whom did he pray? He prayed to himself.

XL.

"This God, who killed God to pacify God," is an excellent quote from Baron de la Hontan's book. You'll find fewer proofs in a hundred massive volumes written pro and contra Christianity, than in the absurdity of these two lines.

XLI.

To say that man is a composite of both strength and weakness, of intelligence and blindness, meanness and greatness, is not to judge him, but simply to define him.

XLII.

Man is as God or nature made him; and God and nature make no mistakes.

XLIII.

What we call "Original Sin" (le péché originel), Ninon de l'Enclos called "the Novel Sin" (le péché original).

XLIV.

It is unrivaled shamelessness to claim that the Gospels harmonize with one another, since some of them contain facts which the rest ignore.

XLV.

Plato thought of his God under three aspects: goodness, wisdom and power. If you don't want to see the Christian trinity there, close your eyes. What we call the *Word* was, almost three thousand years ago, called the *Logos* by the Athenian philosopher.

XLVI.

The divine persons are either three accidents, or three substances. There is no middle way. If they are three accidents, then we are either atheists or deists. If they are three substances, then we are pagans.

XLVII.

God the Father judges men worthy of his eternal vengeance: God the Son judges them worthy of his infinite mercy: the Holy Spirit remains neutral. How can we harmonize this Catholic verbiage with the unity of the divine will?

XLVIII.

Long ago, the theologians were asked to reconcile the dogma of eternal punishment with God's infinite mercy. They're still working on it.

XLIX.

And why punish the guilty, when there is no longer any benefit in his punishment?

L.

He who punishes for his own sake only, is very wicked and very cruel.

LI.

No good father would act the way our Heavenly Father does.

LII.

What proportionality is there between the offender and the offended? What proportionality is there between crime and punishment? What a pile of stupidities and atrocities!

LIII.

And what is he so angry about, this God? And do they not say that I am powerless to do anything, for or against his glory, his peace of mind, his happiness?

LIV.

It is desired that God should burn the wicked, despite their being powerless before Him, in a fire that will last forever; at the same time we would hardly tolerate a father who should give a quick death to his own son, who might compromise his life, his honor, and his fortune!

LV.

O Christians! You have two different ideas of goodness and wickedness, of truth and lies. You are either the most absurd of the dogmatists, or the most outrageous of Pyrrhonists.

LVI.

All the evil a person can do is far from all the evil that is possible: yet, the only person who could possibly deserve an eternal punishment is someone who can commit all the evil that is possible. By making God infinitely vindictive in this way, you are also transforming an earthworm into an infinitely powerful being.

LVII.

To hear a theologian exaggerating the actions of a man who was fashioned by God to be lusty, and who slept with his neighbor's wife, whom God also made pretty and obliging, would we not also expect to hear that the four quarters of the world had been set on fire? Ha! My friend, if you read Marcus Aurelius you will see how much you enrage your God by this illicit and voluptuous rubbing together of two intestines.

LVIII.

The word these atrocious Christians have translated as "eternal" does not mean, in Hebrew, anything more than "lasting." So the dogma of an eternal punishment came from ignorance of Hebrew, as well as the bad temper of a translator.

LIX.

Pascal said, "If your religion is false, you will risk nothing by believing it is true; if it is true, you risk everything by believing it to be false." But any Imam could say the same thing.

LX.

That story where Jesus Christ—i.e., God—was tempted by the Devil is a tale worthy of *The Thousand and One Nights*.

LXI.

I would love for a Christian, best of all a Jansenist, to explain the *cui bono* ("who benefits") of the incarnation. Would it not be best to inflate the number of the damned to infinity, to make best use of this dogma?

LXII.

A young girl lived all alone: one day she received the visit of a young man carrying a bird; she got pregnant; people wondered who the father was... Hmm! It must have been the bird.

LXIII.

But why do the swan of Leda and the little flames of Castor and Pollux make us laugh, but we do not laugh at the dove and the tongues of fire in the Bible?

LXIV.

In the first centuries, there were sixty Gospels, all of which were accepted more or less as equals. Fifty-six of these were rejected for being too childish and clumsy. But are the surviving ones really any better?

LXV.

First God gives a law to men, and then he abolishes it. Is this not like a ruler who makes a mistake, then recognizes it afterwards? Is that what perfect beings do—change their minds?

LXVI.

There are as many kinds of faith as there are religions in the world.

LXVII.

All of the religions are only heresies stemming from deism.

LXVIII.

If man is unhappy without being born guilty, will it not be true that he is destined to enjoy an eternal happiness, without being able, by nature, ever to deserve it?

LXIX.

Those are my thoughts on Christian dogma; I will only leave a quick note about its morality:

In the case of some Catholic father who is convinced that the teachings of the Gospel must be followed to the letter, on pain of what is called Hell: when such a man notes the extreme difficulty in attaining that degree of perfection which human frailty prevents, the best rule of conduct for him would be to seize his child by his feet and smash her against the ground, or even to smother her at birth. By so doing he saves her from any danger of damnation and secures eternal happiness for her.

I maintain that this action, far from being criminal, should be regarded as infinitely praiseworthy, since it comes from paternal love, which requires that every good father must do the best he can for his children.

LXX.

About those religious precepts and societal laws which forbid the murder of innocents: are they not actually quite absurd and even cruel? By killing an innocent person we assure them an infinite happiness, while by letting them live we almost certainly damn them to eternal misery!

LXXI.

Why then, Monsieur De La Condamine, are we allowed to inoculate our children to keep them safe from small pox, but we are not allowed to kill them to keep them safe and secure from Hellfire? You must be joking.

LXXII.

It is enough for truth to win if good people, few as they may be, receive it; but it is not in truth's nature to please many.

UNPUBLISHED THOUGHTS

***

In ancient times on the island of Ternate, it was forbidden for the ordinary people, as well as the priests, to talk about religion.

There was only one temple there; a law expressly forbade a second one. It contained neither altars, nor statues, nor images. A hundred priests, who enjoyed a considerable income, served in this temple.

They neither sang nor spoke, but with a profound silence they indicated, with their finger, a pyramid on which these words were written:

Mortals: worship God, love your brethren, and be useful citizens.

***

A certain man had been betrayed by his children, his wife, and his friends too; faithless associates of his had wasted his fortune and he was driven into poverty. Being filled with hatred and a profound loathing for humanity, he left human society and took refuge in a cave. There, with his fists clenched to his eyes, he said:

"Those vermin! What will I not do to repay their injustices, and make them miserable like they deserve? Oh! If only I could think of something... to fill their heads with a great illusion which they would care about more than they do their own lives—something they'll never be able to wrap their heads around!"

At that instant he leaped out of the cavern, shouting, "God! God!" His voice rang in an echo: "God! God!"

This fearful name was carried from one pole to the other and everywhere it was heard with astonishment. First, men prostrated themselves. Upon rising again, they started to ask each other questions, began to argue, became embittered, resorting to curses and, filled with hatred, ended by cutting each other's throats.

In the end, the fatal wish of the misanthrope was fulfilled. For this has been, and always will be, the history of a Being who is always in equal measure important and incomprehensible.

ON THE SUFFICIENCY OF NATURAL RELIGION

Written in 1747, Published 1770

I.

Natural religion was created either by God or by man. But we cannot allow it to have been manmade, since it provided the foundation for revealed religion.

If it is the work of God, I ask why God would give it to us. The goals of a divine religion must only ever be the knowledge of essential truth, and the practice of important duties. A religion would be unworthy of both God and man if it had any other goals.

Therefore, either God has given us no satisfactory religion—which would be absurd, for this would betray either weakness or malevolence on His part; or God gave man what he required. Therefore, he had no need for supernatural knowledge.

As to the means of fulfilling his duties, it would be absurd to think that man had been refused these; for of these three things: knowledge of dogmas, practice of duties, and the power required to act and believe, if one of them is lacking, the other two are useless.

It would be fruitless for me to learn the dogmas while remaining ignorant of my duties. It is pointless to know my duty, if I misunderstand or do not know the basic truths. It would be pointless to possess knowledge of truths and duties, when the grace of believing and practicing is not also given to me.

I conclude that I have always had all the above; that natural religion left nothing for revealed religion to do, at least nothing essential; therefore, natural religion was not at all insufficient.

II.

If natural religion were insufficient, it would have been insufficient in itself, or relative to man's condition.

Yet, neither of these can be true. A state of insufficiency-in-itself would be a failure on God's part. Its insufficiency relative to man's condition would imply that God was able to make natural religion sufficient, therefore making revealed religion superfluous, by changing the condition of man; which revealed religion will not allow.

Moreover, a religion that is insufficient relative to man's condition will be intrinsically insufficient; since religion is made for man, and every religion which does not place man in a state of paying God His due will be defective in itself.

Now, let none say that since God owes nothing to man, He can, without injustice, grant him whatever He pleases; for that this would render the gift of God pointless and fruitless, two flaws that we could not pardon in man, and which we should not want to criticize in God. Pointless, because God could not thereby aim to obtain from us by this means, that which this means cannot of itself produce. Fruitless, since it is maintained that the means is insufficient to produce any fruit that would be legitimate.

III.

Natural religion was sufficient, if God could not require

anything more from me than what this law stipulated; yet God could not require more from me than this law stipulated, since this law was His own, and since it is only for Him to add or subtract any of its precepts.

Natural religion was sufficient to save those who lived under its law, as much as the Law of Moses did for the Jews and the regime of Christianity for the Christians. The law comprises our obligations, and we cannot be obliged beyond its commandments.

Thus, even if the natural law could be perfected, it was just as sufficient for the first generations, as the same law, perfected, would be for their descendants.

IV.

But, if the natural law were able to be perfected by the Law of Moses, and this one, by Christianity, then why is the Christian law not possibly going to be perfected by a new one, which God has not yet deigned to bestow on humanity?

V.

If the natural law had been perfected, this would have been either by truths that were revealed to us, or by new virtues that the people had previously ignored. Yet, neither of these two can be true. The revealed law contains no moral precept which I do not find commended and practiced under natural law; therefore, revelation has taught us nothing new in morality. The revealed law has not brought us any new truth; for what is a truth, if not a proposition relative to an object, conceived in terms that present me with clear ideas, and whose relationships I can clearly perceive? Yet revealed religion has not brought us anything like that. What it actually adds beyond natural law is five or six propositions that are about as intelligible to me they would be if they were written in ancient

Carthaginian, since the ideas represented by the terms, and the connections between these ideas, completely elude me.

Both the ideas represented by the terms and their connections elude me; for, without these two conditions, the revealed propositions either cease to be mysteries, or are patently absurd. Take for example, this revealed proposition: *the sons of Adam have all been guilty, from birth, of the sin of this first father*. A proof that the ideas attached to these terms and their connections escape me in this proposition, is that if I substitute for the name of Adam that of Peter, or of Paul, and then I say: the children of Paul have all been guilty, since birth, of the fall of their father, the proposition becomes a plain and manifest absurdity.

From this, and from what precedes it, it follows that revealed religion has taught us nothing about morality; and what it gave us for dogma, can be reduced to five or six unintelligible propositions, and which, by consequence, we cannot accept as truths. For if you teach a rube, who knows no Latin and even less logic, the verse: *Asserit A, negat E, verum generaliter ambo*, would you believe you revealed a new truth to him? Is it not in the nature of all truth to be clear and to have the power to enlighten the mind? Revealed propositions cannot have these properties. They clearly contain, or it is clear that they contain a truth, but they are obscure; from which it follows that everything inferred from them will share this same obscurity; for a conclusion can never be clearer than a principle.

VI.

That religion is best, which best agrees with the goodness of God. Natural religion agrees with the goodness of God, for one of the traits of the goodness of God, is to exclude no person. Yet natural law best fulfills this requirement; for it is natural law that we can truly call the light which everyone brings with them from the womb.

VII.

That religion is best which best agrees with the justice of God. Yet natural religion or law is, of all religions, the one which best agrees with justice. Men, presented at God's judgment bar, will be judged by some law; if God judges men by the natural law He will do no injustice to any of them, given that they are all born under this law. On the other hand, if God were to judge men by any other law, which was far from being known to all of them, many will unjustly fall foul of this justice. It follows then, either that God will judge everyone according to whatever law they knew about, or if He judges all of them by one universal law, this can only be the natural law, which is equally known to all, and therefore obliges everyone equally.

VIII.

Moreover, I would state that: there are people whose intelligence is so reduced that the universality of feelings is the only witness within their reach; it follows that the Christian religion is not made for such men, since it does not have this witness for them, and consequently they are either condemned to follow no religion, or to fall into the natural religion, the goodness of which is accepted by everyone.

IX.

"Gauls, to whom if any, do you yield in courage? To the Romans. Parthians, after you, who are the most courageous men? The Romans. Africans, whom would you fear, if you were to fear anyone? The Romans."

"When Cicero," said the author of *The Philosophical Thoughts*, "wanted to prove that the Romans were the most belligerent people on Earth, he cleverly drew this affirmation from the mouths of their enemies. "Gauls, to whom if any, do you yield in courage? To the Romans. Parthians, after you, who are the most courageous men? The Romans. Africans, whom would you fear, if you were to fear anyone? The Romans. Let us, following his example, interrogate each of the religions," said the author of *The Thoughts*, "in the same way:

"Chinese, what religion would be best, if not your own? Natural religion. Muslims, what faith would you embrace, should you ever swear off Muhammad? Naturalism. Christians, which is the true religion, if it is not Christianity? The religion of the Jews. But you, O Jews, which is the true religion, if Judaism is false? Naturalism.

"Now those," continue both Cicero and the author of *The Thoughts*, "who are awarded second place unanimously, and who do not in turn yield first place to anyone deserve, without contest, first place."

X.

That religion is the most reasonable in the eyes of reasonable beings, which treats them most as reasonable beings, since it does not teach them to believe anything beyond reason, or anything that contradicts it.

XI.

In preference to the rest, that religion should be followed which offers the most divine traits; and natural religion is, among all religions, the one which offers the most divine traits; for there is no divine trait in the any other sect which is not also recognizable in natural religion; and it has some which the rest lack, namely: immutability and universality.

XII.

What is a sufficient and universal grace? That which is bestowed on all mankind, with which they are always able to fulfill their duties, and by which they often do fulfill them.

What could a sufficient religion look like, if not like our natural religion, this religion that is given to all mankind and by which they can always fulfill their duties and often do fulfill them? From this it follows that not only is natural religion not insufficient to do this, but that properly speaking, it is the only religion that could do it; and that it would be infinitely more absurd to deny the need for a universal and sufficient religion, than for a universal and sufficient grace. Yet, we cannot deny the need for a universal and sufficient grace, without falling into insurmountable difficulties, nor consequently that of a sufficient and universal religion. And natural religion is the only one that has this quality.

XIII.

If natural religion is defective in any way, two things would follow from this: either it never has been faithfully followed by anyone who did not know any other religion, or those who had faithfully observed the only law they knew about, have been punished, or they have been rewarded. If they have been rewarded, then their religion is sufficient, since it brought about the same effect as the Christian religion. It would be absurd to say that they were punished. It is unbelievable that any of them had been faithful observers of their law. This would be to enclose all morality in a tiny corner of the Earth, or to punish a great many honest people.

XIV.

Among all the religions, that should be preferred, whose truth has more proofs going for it, and the fewest contradictions against it? Natural religion is well described here, for no objection can be raised against it, and all the other religions agree in advocating its truth.

XV.

How could its insufficiency be proven? First, on the basis of the fact that this insufficiency has been recognized by all other religions; second, because the knowledge of the true and the practice of the good have been lacking in even the wisest of naturalists. These proofs are falsified. As to the first part, if all the religions agree that it is insufficient, it is apparently because the naturalists don't agree with them. In this case, naturalism is like any other religion which its adherents claim is the best one, in contrast to all the other faiths.

As to the second part, it is well known that since the advent of revealed religion, neither our knowledge of God, nor of our duties, have been augmented. Since all of God's intelligible attributes are plain to all, while His alleged and unintelligible attributes add nothing to our understanding; we ourselves, since self-knowledge communicated everything to us regarding our nature and our duties; our duties were already shown in the books of pagan philosophers, and our nature is forever inscrutable, since what some would claim to teach us which is beyond philosophy, comes in the form of propositions which are either unintelligible, or which sound absurd *prima facie,* and we conclude nothing against naturalism from the way naturalists behave.

It is as easy that natural religion should be good, and that its precepts should have been badly observed, as it is for the Christian religion to be true, no matter how infinitely many bad Christians there have been.

XVI.

If God owed mankind no tools fit to fulfill their duties, at least His nature did not allow Him to give them bad tools. Yet, an insufficient tool would be a bad tool; for the first distinctive trait of a good tool is its fitness for some task.

But, if natural religion were absolutely sufficient with its universal grace or enlightenment, to support a man while he travels the path of morality, who would tell me that such a thing has not come to us? Moreover, revealed religion could only bring about the best situation, and not by absolute necessity; if a naturalist does good deeds, these would have infinitely more merit than the Christian, since they have both done the same thing, but the naturalist with infinitely less encouragement.

XVII.

But I demand to be told sincerely which of the two religions is easier to follow, the natural religion or the Christian religion. If it is the natural religion, as I believe and have never been able to doubt, Christianity is then only a superfluous burden, not a grace; it is only a very difficult way to do something that can be done quite easily. If you say the Christian law, note my response: a law is harder to follow, as its precepts are numerous and rigid. You may reply that the encouragements to follow them are stronger in comparison to the encouragements to the natural law, and that the precepts of these two laws are similar in their number and their difficulty. But who is doing this calculation and this compensation? Don't tell me that it is Jesus Christ and his Church, since only Christians believe in such, and you have not yet lured me into your camp; and you cannot simply convert me by presupposing this in your arguments. So look for other arguments.

XVIII.

Everything that had a beginning must end; and anything that had no beginning will have no end. Christianity had a beginning; Judaism had a beginning; yet there is no single religion on Earth whose date of origin is not known, aside from the natural religion; therefore it alone will have no ending; all others will pass away.

XIX.

Between these two religions, we should prefer the one which is more obviously of divine origin, and fewer marks of human origins. Natural law is plainly from God; it is infinitely more obvious that it came from God, than that other religions had human origins: for there is no objection against its divinity, and it needs no proofs; meanwhile we can make a thousand objections against the divine origins of the rest, and they require an infinity of proofs before we can believe in them.

XX.

The religion is preferable which is most analogous to the nature of God; but natural law is most analogous to the nature of God. It is in God's nature to be incorruptible, and incorruptibility is displayed better by the natural law than by any other, because the precepts of the other laws are written in books subject to all the mishaps of human history, such as excision, misinterpretation, unintelligibility of language, etc. Since the natural religion is written in the heart, it is sheltered from all these perils; if it has some revolution to fear from prejudice and passion, it shares these dangers with all other forms of worship, and these are also exposed to sources of change that are peculiar to themselves.

XXI.

Either natural religion is good, or it is evil. If it is good, that is enough; I ask nothing more. If it is evil, the revealed religions are built on a flawed foundation.

XXII.

If there were some reason to prefer the Christian religion to natural religion, it would be the fact that it offered further knowledge about God and man. Yet there is none to be had: Christianity, instead of clarifying, opens the door to an infinite multitude of obscurities and difficulties.

If we asked the natural-religionist why man suffers in this world, he would respond, "I don't know." If we ask a Christian the same question, he would give you some enigma or an absurd response. Ought we to prefer mystery over ignorance? Or maybe they amount to the same thing?

Why should man suffer in this world? "It is a mystery," says the Christian. "It is a mystery," says the naturalist. But note that the Christian's response quickly dissolves into the same thing. If he says, "man suffers because his ancestor sinned," and you persist: "and why should a grandson have to pay for the stupid mistake of his grandfather?" He says, "That is a mystery."

"Oh?" I would respond to the Christian: "so why not just start out by saying, as I do, that if man suffers without apparent cause, it is a mystery? Don't you see that you are explaining this phenomenon just like the Chinese explained the suspension of the world in the air?

Q: "What holds the world up?"

A: "A big elephant."

Q: "And what's the elephant standing on?"

A: "A turtle."

Q: "And what's under the turtle?"

A: "I don't know."

Oh my friend, why don't you leave the elephants and turtles alone and just confess your ignorance from the start?

XXIII.

That religion is preferable above all which can only do good and never evil. But the natural law is engraved on everyone's heart. They will all find that they carry the disposition to find this law in themselves, whereas all other religions, which are based on principles foreign to humanity and, consequently, necessarily unintelligible to most people, necessarily lead to dissension among men. Moreover, whatever is confirmed by experience should be accepted as true. But it is from experience that the religions claimed to be revealed have caused a thousand misfortunes, set mankind at odds, and painted every country with bloody hues. Yet natural religion has yet to extract a single tear from mankind.

XXIV.

We must reject any system which spreads doubt about universal benevolence, and the constant equity of God. Yet, the system which considers natural religion insufficient, casts doubt on the universal benevolence and constant equity of God. In their systems I only see a being who feels very limited affections for his children, whose planning is volatile, who restricts his blessings to a small portion of humanity, who now disapproves of the same behavior he commanded previously; if men cannot be saved outside the Christian religion, then for the unsaved, God is like to a mother who only gives her milk to one or two of many children. On the contrary, if natural religion is sufficient, then everything is right in the universe, and I will respect the true benevolence and equity of God.

XXV.

Could it not be said that all the religions of the world are simply deviations from natural religion, and that the Jews, the Christians, the Muslims, and even the Pagans are only heretical and schismatic naturalists?

XXVI.

Consequently, could we not claim that the natural religion is the only religion that actually exists? For, if we take the follower of any religion and interrogate them, soon you will discover that among the dogmas of his religion there are some which he believes less than others or even denies; not to speak of a great many others that he either does not understand or which he interprets in his own idiosyncratic way. Speak to a second member of that religion, ask the very same questions, and you will find exactly the same as before, with the one difference, that that which he does not doubt at all and which he believes, is precisely what his fellow member denies, and what he does not understand, is what the other believes he understands very well indeed; the parts which embarrass him cause no difficulty at all to his fellow, and that they will fail to agree about what is worthy of interpretation. However, all men march together to the base of the same altars; they seem to think alike, but they hardly agree on anything. Such that, if all people would reciprocally sacrifice the beliefs they disagree about, they would almost be naturalists right away, and would leave their various temples to join with the deists.

XXVII.

The truth of the natural religion stands against the truth of other religions in the same way that:

The witness that I get for myself stands against the testimony that I hear from someone else;

That which I feel stands against what I am informed about by someone else;

That which is impressed on me by the finger of God stands against that which vain, superstitious and deceitful men have written on scrolls or carved in stone;

That which I carry inside myself and find is everywhere the same, stands against what is outside myself, and changes with the environs;

That which has never been, nor is nor ever will truly be doubted, stands against that which, far from being believed, has never been known, or has ceased to be, or has never been known, or has ceased to be, or is not, or is rightly rejected as false;

That which neither time nor men have abolished nor ever will abolish, against that which passes as a shadow;

That which reconciles the civilized man with the barbarian, the Christian with the infidel, the pagan with the devotee of Jehovah, those who worship Jupiter with those who worship God, the philosopher with the masses, the savant with the ignoramus; the old man with the child, the wisest man with the madman; stands against that which divides father from son, raises the weapon one man against another, exposes the savant and sage to hatred and persecution by the ignorant and the fanatics, and from time to time soaks the Earth with the blood of all;

That which is held to be holy, august and sacred by all peoples on Earth, against that which is cursed by all, with the exception of one only;

That which has compelled hymns, praises and canticles to rise up towards heaven, against that which has spawned anathemas, impieties, execration and blasphemies;

That which teaches that we all form part of a single, immense family with God as its first father, against that which teaches that humanity must be subdivided into small bands possessed by swarms of wild and wicked demons, who place sword in their right hand, and a torch in the left, and which whip them up to murder, ravages and destruction.

The coming centuries will continue to brighten the first of these with the fairest hues; the other will continue to darken itself with the blackest shades. While the religions of humanity continue to shame themselves by their extravagance and crimes, natural religion will crown itself with a new burst of light, and humanity may at last set its sights on it, and it will set them on their feet; then they will become a single society; they will get rid of these bizarre laws which appear to have been dreamed up only to make men wicked and guilty; they will heed only the voice of nature and they will finally start once again to be simple and virtuous.

O mortals! How did you ever become so miserable? How I pity and love you! Overwhelming commiseration and tenderness have always led me; and I have promised you a happiness which you have forever fled and rejected.

RULING OF THE PARLEMENT OF PARIS REGARDING THE *PHILOSOPHICAL THOUGHTS,* 1746

AN EXTRACT FROM THE RECORDS OF THE *PARLEMENT,* 7 July 1746

On this day the *Gens du Roi* entered, and Master Pierre-Paul Gilbert de Voisins, Lawyer of the *Seigneur Roi*, acting as spokesman, said:

That, in light of the extent to which license has been carried in the writings in which the public has for some time now been inundated by clandestine printing, they often regret having remained silent, but that sometimes it is preferable to abandon to obscurity certain libels which are more worthy of contempt than indignation. But as this silence, when it seems to last too long, may send the message of impunity instead; that, moreover, there are objects, the scandal of which is all too visible, and which of themselves require public condemnation.

That, of such are the two works which we believe ourselves obliged to remand to the Court. The one is entitled, *Histoire naturelle de l'Ame*, which on the pretext of a profound study of the nature and characteristics of the human spirit, in this way strives to annihilate it; by reducing it to matter, it saps the foundations of all religion and all virtue.

That the other, under the title of *Philosophical Thoughts*, presents to anxious and rash minds the venom of the most criminal and absurd opinions of which the depravation of human reason is capable, and by a feigned uncertainty, places all religions almost on the same level, ending by recognizing none of them.

That both the sanctity of religion and the plainest interests of civil society are equally outraged by such culpable attacks against them. That anyone who dares so audaciously to attack what is most sacred, will no longer be held back by any restraint; that it is to become the enemy of humanity to proclaim to men that their passions must be the only rule of their conduct.

And let the zeal of their ministry not be restricted to acting against these works; let it also extend to the pursuit of their authors, and make them suffer a punishment whose example will terrify their peers.

The following objects are left to the Court: their written Conclusions, along with the copies of the two works which they believe they should remand thereto.

The Gens du Roi retired. Two books were examined; the first was entitled: *Histoire naturelle de l'Ame, translated from the English of Mr. Charp. by the late M. H** of the Academy of the Sciences: Participem lethi quoque convenit esse*, printed at the Hague by Jean Neaulme, Bookseller, 1745. The second was entitled: *Philosophical Thoughts: Piscis hic non est omnium*, printed at the Hague, at the expense of the Company, 1746. Together with the written conclusions of the King's *Procureur Général*.

The matter was deliberated:

The COURT has ordained and ordains that the two above-mentioned books are to be shredded and burned in the Court of the Palace, at the foot of the great staircase of the same by the Executioner of High Justice, as scandalous and as contrary to religion and good morals. Express injunctions and prohibitions are to be made to all booksellers, printers, peddlers, and all others from printing, selling, retailing, or otherwise distributing them in any manner whatsoever, on pain of corporal punishment. Anyone who is in possession of any copies is enjoined to deliver them immediately to the Civil Registry of the Court, to have them suppressed.

The Royal *Procureur Général* is hereby authorized to conduct an investigation regarding those who have composed, printed, sold, retailed or distributed the above-mentioned books, in presence of Master Aimé-Jean-Jacques Severt, Counselor, whom the Court has commissioned, by the witnesses who will be in this city; and in presence of the Criminal Lieutenants of the bailiwicks and *sénéchaussées*, and other judges of royal cases, in pursuit of substitutes for the Royal *Procureur Général* these domains, for any witnesses who find themselves in these places. The Royal *Procureur Général* is authorized to this effect, to obtain and have published *Monitoires* in legal form; as for the information that is gathered, reported and communicated to the Royal *Procureur Général*, that he should make such conclusions, and that the Court ordain whatsoever shall pertain thereto:

It is ordained that collated copies of the present ruling are to be sent to the bailiwicks and *sénéchaussées* of these jurisdictions, to be read, published and registered there, and the representatives of the Royal *Procureur Général* are enjoined to carry this out, and to report thereupon to the Court within a month. CONCLUDED in *Parlement* on the seventh of July one thousand seven hundred forty-six. Signed, YSABEAU.

On the above-mentioned day of the seventh of July one thousand seven hundred forty-six, at the end of the Court's session, in execution of the above-mentioned ruling, the two books therein mentioned have been shredded and cast into the fire by the Executioner of High Justice, at the base of the great staircase of the palace, in presence of myself, MARIE-DAGOBERT YSABEAU, one of the three first and principal representatives of the Great Chamber, with two Constables of the same Court in attendance also.

Signed, YSABEAU.

IN PARIS, BY PIERRE GUILLAUME SIMON, PRINTER FOR THE *PARLEMENT*, RUE DE LA HARPE, AT L'HERCULE, 1746.